City of Angels

In and Around Los Angeles

By Julie Jaskol & Brian Lewis ❀ Illustrated by Elisa Kleven

*In the memory of my mother, Lorraine Art Schneider,
who filled my L.A. childhood with art and love. —E.K.*

To the children of Los Angeles, especially Rose and Walker —J.J. & B.L.

Many thanks to our L.A. families who helped us so much: Stan and Sally Schneider, Carol Schneider, Susie Messenger, Sylvia Morales, Cathy Davies, Anita Jaskol, and Stan and Jann Jaskol. Thanks also to Paddy Calistro, Scott McAuley, Jim Schneeweis and Chuck Morrell at Angel City Press, graphic designer Amy Inouye of Future Studio, and Judy Graeme and Kevin Roderick.

Acknowledgments

We would also like to extend our thanks to: Afrikan Color Scheme; Jay Aldrich, Autry National Center; Elayne Alexander, Venice Historical Society; Elena Allen; Armando, Mariachi Photo Studio; Catherine Babcock, Music Center; Linda Barth, City of Los Angeles Department of Recreation and Parks; Jeffrey Baskin, Paramount Pictures; Brian Breyé, Museum in Black; California Lawyers for the Arts; Canter's Delicatessen; Canton Poultry; Capitol Records; Casa del Músico; CBS; Christine Chrisman, Los Angeles Dodgers; City of Los Angeles Department of Cultural Affairs; Darlene Daniels, Pages Books for Children; Du-par's Restaurant; Doug Dutton, Dutton's Books; Mike Eberts, *Griffith Park: A Centennial History*; Filomena Eriman, Grand Central Market; William Estrada, El Pueblo de Los Angeles Historical Monument; Greg Fischer; Pamela Fisher; James Fugate, Eso Won Books; Louise Gabriel, Santa Monica Historical Society; Marty Geimer, Beverly Hills Historical Society; Mark Greenfield, Watts Towers; Eugene Grigsby, UCLA; Chris Hills, Los Angeles Natural History Museum; The Hollywood Bowl; Hong Ning Co.; Thacher Hurd; Jacquie Israel, Storyopolis; The Israel Levin Senior Center; Lucy Jones, U.S. Geological Survey; Sachiko Kimura, Little Tokyo Business Association; Chris M. Komai, Japanese American National Museum; Kongo Square; The Honorable Tom LaBonge; Dr. Lanier, Kids' Dental Kare; Michael Laxineta; Leimert Park Eyewear; Susan Malk, the White Rabbit Children's Bookstore; Christy McAvoy, Historic Resources Group; Gary McCarthy, *Los Angeles Independent*; Cindy McNaughton, Central Library; Mann's Chinese Theatre; Mariachi Appliance Store; John Michael, Plaza Commons, Inc., at California Plaza; Eugene W. Moy, Chinese Historical Society of Southern California; Danny Muñoz, Echo Park Historical Society; Musso & Frank Grill; NBC; Judy Nelson, Mrs. Nelson's Toy & Book Shop; Adolfo Nodal; Phil Orland, Angels Gate Park; José Luis Orozco; The Page Museum at the La Brea Tar Pits; Jan Palchikoff; Mark Panatier, Farmers Market; Philippe French Dipped Sandwiches; Jean Bruce Poole, El Pueblo de Los Angeles Historical Monument; Mary Rainwater; Mr. Ramen; Catherine Rice; The Honorable Mark Ridley-Thomas; Hitoshi Sameshima, Japanese American National Museum; Santa Cecilia Restaurant; Santa Monica Pier Restoration Corporation; Joy Sekimura; Ingeborg Sepp, Caltech; Avra Shapiro and Liebe Geft, Simon Wiesenthal Center Museum of Tolerance; Jody Shapiro, Adventures for Kids; Michael Stone, UCLA; Cooke Sunoo; Yasuyuki Suzuki, Miyako Hotel; Betty Takeuchi, San Marino Toy & Book Shoppe; Mark Teichrow, *Los Angeles Times*; Alex Uhl, A Whale of a Tale; Earl Underwood, Leimert Park Fine Art Gallery; The Vision Theater; Msgr. Francis J. Weber, Archdiocese of Los Angeles Archival Center; Sydney Weisman and David Hamlin; John Welborne, Angels Flight Railway Foundation; Earl White, The Dance Collective; Gloria Williams, Norton Simon Museum; Larry Wilson, *Pasadena Star-News*; Wonder Bakery; Cy Wong, Chinese Historical Society of Southern California; Mike Woo; Cynthia Wornham, The J. Paul Getty Trust; and Liana Yamasaki, Tournament of Roses.

Angels Flight and the images of the Angels Flight Railway and cars are trademarks of the Angels Flight Railway Company and are used with permission. The Hollywood Sign and the Hollywood Walk of Fame, trademarks of the Hollywood Chamber of Commerce, are used with permission.

Title page: The largest lotus bed outside China blooms in Echo Park Lake, and every July the lotuses form the backdrop for the Lotus Festival, celebrating Asian and Pacific Island cultures. Los Angeles' first suburban neighborhood took root along Echo Park Lake. When downtown got too crowded in the 1880s, people created a more peaceful residential community in Echo Park, building Victorian homes, some of which have been preserved in all their gingerbread glory on Carroll Avenue. Generation after generation has sought the perfect suburb by creating new neighborhoods and cities in all directions around downtown. Dodger Stadium crowned a hill in Echo Park in 1962, and most of the downtown skyline and the freeways that ring it rose in the 1960s and 1970s, when redevelopment changed the landscape dramatically.

Contents

ACP

ANGEL CITY PRESS

Introduction

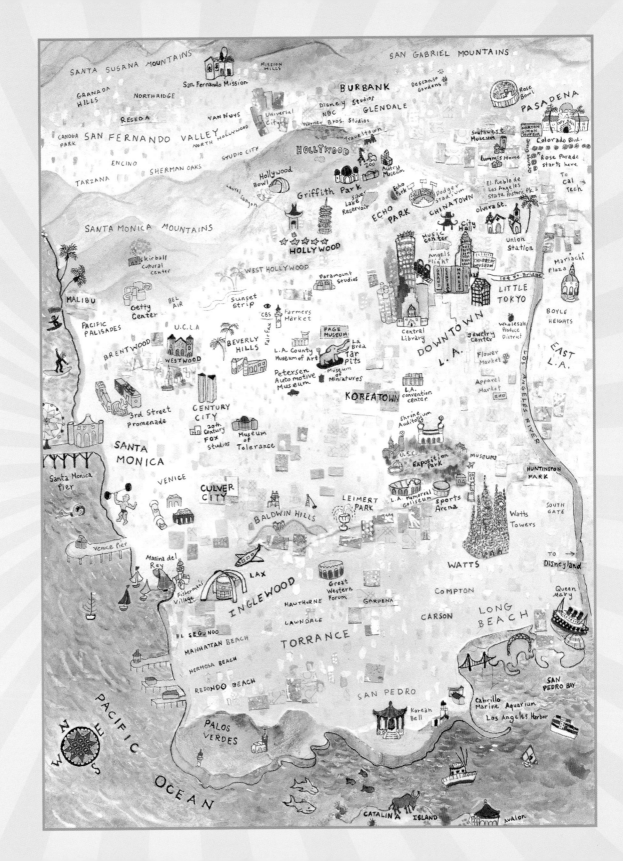

On a hot summer day in 1769, an expedition of Spanish soldiers and Franciscan friars set up camp by a river on a broad plain that would later come to be known as the Los Angeles basin. Having the day before celebrated the Feast of Our Lady Queen of the Angels, a Catholic holiday, they named their campsite *El Pueblo de la Reina de Los Angeles*—The Town of the Queen of the Angels. By 1850, when the campsite had grown to a small town and California had been admitted to the Union, the name had shrunk to *Los Angeles*—Spanish for "The Angels." Isolated from the rest of the nation by mountain ranges to the north, east, and south, and the vast Mojave Desert beyond them, Los Angeles lay near the Pacific Ocean, but had no natural harbor. It didn't even have a reliable source of fresh water for drinking or irrigation. Not long after the Spanish explorers camped on its green banks, the river flooded and changed its course, running south to the sea in far-off San Pedro. The Los Angeles basin was left dry and dusty.

Yet a city grew because the people determinedly remade the land. By the early twentieth century, railroads linked Los Angeles to the rest of the nation; a port in San Pedro connected it to the rest of the world; and a pipeline from Owens Valley in the north supplied a steady flow of water. Los Angeles' balmy climate and the vast possibilities of its wide open spaces irresistibly pulled people from older, colder cities in the East and around the world. Expanding without the rigid grids of planned communities, Los Angeles sprawled this way and that, eventually stretching some 465 square miles, gobbling up smaller cities in its path. Pasadena, Santa Monica, and Beverly Hills managed to keep their independent city governments, but Hollywood, Venice, and other smaller towns became neighborhoods of Los Angeles. Today more than four million residents make

it the second largest city in the U.S. The city of Los Angeles is contained within Los Angeles County, which covers more than 4,000 square miles and consists of eighty-eight separate cities and more than ten million people. The region boasts the world's highest rate of immigration, particularly from Asia and Latin America.

Streets change their character from block to block in Los Angeles. Teeming, densely packed neighborhoods can quickly give way to quiet, lush areas where huge homes hide behind tall hedges. Cultures visually blend and collide. Storefront signs written in Armenian dissolve into signs in Korean or Thai. Mediterranean-style houses with red-tiled roofs are flanked by English country cottages and unique "dingbat" apartment buildings, little more than boxes on stilts.

Some people sum up the city in easy-to-grasp clichés: convertibles, palm trees, cell phones, and movie stars; or by its natural disasters, earthquakes and annual brushfires that threaten to wipe Los Angeles off its canyons and hillsides. Writers have long tried to distill Los Angeles. Humorist Dorothy Parker sniffed dismissively that "Los Angeles is seventy-two suburbs in search of a city." Historian Carey McWilliams said it was like "a ringside seat at the circus." Novelist Raymond Chandler declared "Los Angeles was just a big dry sunny place with ugly homes and no style, but good-hearted and peaceful."

This book does not try to offer a complete view of Los Angeles. It presents a collection of neighborhoods and landmarks that offer some insight into the city's history, diversity, and range. Our apologies if we left out your favorite places. We left out many of our favorite places, too. The selections take you through a year in Los Angeles, beginning with Chinese New Year in Chinatown. An angel or two is tucked in each large picture for good measure—see if you can find them all.

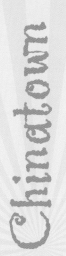

Chinatown

The New Year roars into Chinatown each winter with the colorful Dragon Parade down Broadway. In the Chinese zodiac, the powerful dragon brings the four blessings of riches, harmony, virtue, and longevity. The dragon has been dancing down these streets for more than one hundred years, since Chinatown was a jumble of narrow dirt roads. Beginning in the mid-1800s, Chinese immigrants working in the gold mines and on railroads moved south and settled in the northeastern part of downtown Los Angeles. Others came from China to join them in a new life in a new land. They created a bustling neighborhood jam-packed with stores

and restaurants that reminded people of their homeland.

That first Chinatown fell to the bulldozer in the 1930s so the city could build its new railway terminal. With its heavy wooden beams and gilded ceilings, Union Station stands majestically, but it came at the cost of a lively community. In 1938, Chinatown rebuilt itself a few blocks to the northwest in a more open style suited to the times, with plazas and broad, straight streets. Many of the original stores and restaurants survive, run by descendants of the first proprietors. Chinatown today serves as a center of Cambodian and Vietnamese commerce as well as Chinese.

Every year on the day before Easter Sunday, Olvera Street and the old Plaza go to the dogs—and cats, goats, pigs, lizards, and snakes. For the Blessing of the Animals, hundreds of people visit this historic street near the site of the Spanish settlement of *El Pueblo de la Reina de Los Angeles,* or The Town of the Queen of the Angels. In 1780, the Spanish governor offered land, horses, plows, and tools, plus ten *pesos* a month, to any farmer who would settle the new *pueblo* as a colony of Spain. The following year, eleven families of mixed Spanish, African, and Indian heritage arrived. They built the *zanja madre,* or mother ditch, to bring water from the nearby Los Angeles River. Farms and ranches flourished, and Los Angeles grew.

In 1926, a woman named Christine Sterling was shocked to see that Olvera Street had become a dirty alley, its buildings on the verge of collapse. She launched a campaign to save it, and on Easter Sunday in 1930, the street opened as a Mexican marketplace. The Blessing of the Animals began as part of her effort to reintroduce a touch of authentic Mexican culture.

"We bless these animals for all they have done," a priest says, sprinkling holy water on each animal's head. "And for tendering a service to the human race."

Little Tokyo

KOYASAN BUDDHIST TEMPLE

You walk through history as you walk along First Street in Little Tokyo. Imprinted on the sidewalk are the words of generations of Japanese immigrants and the names and dates of the many businesses that have lined the street since 1885. By 1908, so many Japanese had settled in this downtown community that their American-born neighbors called it Little Tokyo.

World War II tragically interrupted the flow of life on First Street. At war with Japan, the U.S. government ordered the imprisonment of all West Coast residents of Japanese ancestry. Images of suitcases stamped into the First Street sidewalk recall this painful forced relocation. After three long years in desert prison camps, Japanese Americans returned to Little Tokyo in 1945 and reclaimed their community. Today noodle shops, Buddhist temples, and gardens form the backdrop for both daily life and special events. People come to Little Tokyo from all over to celebrate their customs and history. One such celebration is Children's Day, when carp flags fly to honor the world's children.

The largest city park in the nation, Griffith Park sprawls across more than four thousand acres of hillside—nearly six times as big as New York City's Central Park and four times larger than Golden Gate Park in San Francisco. From the top of the park's brush-covered mountains, hikers can see the entire Los Angeles basin stretching south. In the canyon below, visitors can cool off near a stream lined with lush green ferns. And in between are rolling lawns where families picnic and play in the big, shared backyard that is Griffith Park.

"Public parks are the safety valve of great cities," said Griffith J. Griffith, an eccentric mil-

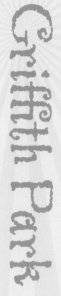

lionaire who donated the park to the people of Los Angeles in 1896. After looking through a telescope at nearby Mount Wilson, Griffith resolved to build an observatory in the park. "If all mankind could look through that telescope, it would revolutionize the world," he said.

With its three copper-covered domes and commanding presence overlooking the city, the Griffith Observatory quickly became one of Los Angeles' most recognizable monuments. Just as Griffith intended, gazing at the stars or hiking in the park can make you forget you're in the second-largest city in the United States.

The lacy, delicate spires of the Watts Towers rise dreamily above the railroad tracks, chain-link fences, and small bungalows of the surrounding South Los Angeles neighborhood. Nearly ten stories high, the towers are the work of one man: Simon Rodia. He toiled alone for more than three decades, without scaffolding, welding torches, or a formal plan—only the graceful vision in his mind.

Every night after work as a stonemason and on the weekends, he built fanciful structures made of steel rods and wrapped them in wire mesh. Section by section, he covered the mesh with wet cement and into it pressed colorful bits and pieces of things he found. Climbing the towers like trees, Rodia adorned them with pieces of green and blue bottle glass, seashells, tiles, mirrors, and plates. He etched hearts, designs, and words into the walls and floors. In his solitary, painstaking way, he also built a ship, a gazebo, birdbaths, walkways, fountains, and a sculpted "cactus garden."

No one knows why Rodia began his labor of love, and no one knows why he stopped. In 1955 he deeded the towers to a neighbor who, as a child, had brought him dishes and bottles to use in his work. Rodia moved to Northern California, where he lived alone, shunning attention, and never saw his towers again. Asked years later why he built the towers, Rodia said simply, "I set out to do something big, and I did."

The sixteen thousand rosebushes in the Exposition Park Rose Garden make this the most fragrant spot in town—and one of the most photographed. Along with the blossoms come dozens of photographers, taking pictures of families posing for keepsakes.

When the park opened south of downtown in 1872, it was called Agricultural Park, and farmers displayed their harvests there. Horses, dogs, and even camels competed along a race-track that lay where the rosebushes bloom today.

As Los Angeles spread southward, the park area became more fashionable. The University of Southern California, built in 1880, attracted distinguished scholars. Soon the city's most influ-

ential families moved into the neighborhood, and they didn't like the racing or gambling that came with the racetrack. In 1913, they replaced it with a garden, and the park became a cultural center with grand museums.

Today a fighter jet pops out of the wall of the Aerospace Museum. The California African American Museum chronicles the black experience in America. Dioramas featuring lifelike stuffed mammals, reptiles, and birds line the halls of the Museum of Natural History and, at the California Science Center, visitors can explore the wonders of our world.

Where cars whiz by today on Wilshire Boulevard, mammoths and saber-toothed cats once roamed. Now all that remains of the Ice Age mammals that lived there as far back as forty thousand years ago can be found inside the Page Museum and deep within nearby pits of tar ("tar" is *brea* in Spanish).

Since the early 1900s, scientists have recovered millions of fossils, along with the nine-thousand-year-old human skull and partial skeleton of a woman—the only human remains ever found in the pits. All these things were preserved in the sticky asphalt produced by a vast, subterranean sea of petroleum that oozed to the surface during warm weather, year after year for thirty thousand years. Rainwater collected on top of the tar, and when animals came to drink, they got stuck in the goo. They died from starvation, or were killed by predators, and their bones slowly sank into the muck. Today, a landscaped tar pit in front of the museum features life-sized statues of mammoths struggling to break free of the tar's grip.

A leafy park connects the Page Museum with the Los Angeles County Museum of Art, or LACMA, the largest art museum in the western U.S., which includes The Pavilion for Japanese Art and one of the most significant collections of Islamic art in the world.

GEORGE C. PAGE MUSEUM
LA BREA DISCOVERIES

ENTRANCE

For generations, Angelenos have made the neighboring coastal city of Santa Monica, just west of L.A., their playground. In the mid-1800s, people endured a daylong buggy ride from Los Angeles to camp on the wide, sandy beach and bathe in the ocean. By the turn of the twentieth century, hundreds of thousands of passengers took the streetcar to the beach each year. They came to stroll along gigantic piers jutting into the ocean, and to enjoy the dance halls, indoor salt water swimming pools, roller coasters, and funhouses along the beach. Today Santa Monica Pier, built in 1909, houses a new amusement park and an old merry-go-round with hand-

carved horses and the oldest organ in the United States, constructed in 1900.

In 1904, an ambitious entrepreneur named Abbot Kinney transformed salt marshes next to Santa Monica into a replica of Venice, Italy, complete with authentic Italian boatmen steering imported gondolas along a series of canals. Eager to have its own shoreline, the city of Los Angeles consolidated with Venice in 1926 and, over the protests of some residents, paved most of the canals. Today the canals that remain have been restored, and ducks and boaters once again paddle along the quiet waters.

Paramount Pictures

Hollywood

Hollywood first became famous not for its movie stars but for its bananas, pineapples, and lemons. Even in winter, tropical fruit thrived under the sunny skies and ocean breezes of the unique temperate zone at the base of the Santa Monica Mountains. Beginning in 1900, tourists came to marvel at Hollywood's gardens and soak up the sun.

In 1907, the warm weather attracted a movie company from back East. Early movie companies needed plenty of sunlight; during dark, snowy winters it was impossible to film. Hollywood's climate promised year-round filmmaking, and the nearby oceans, mountains, and desert provided scenery that could double for almost anywhere else in the world. Other film companies soon followed, and Hollywood's orchards and fields disappeared as movie sets rose in their place. By 1920, Hollywood studios were producing most of the world's popular films, and stars ranked as its biggest exports.

Tourists fit their hands and feet into the impressions left by celebrities in the courtyard of Grauman's Chinese Theatre. Engraved stars bearing famous names decorate the sidewalk on the "Walk of Fame." And the stars in the sky shine down on music lovers at the Hollywood Bowl.

In Los Angeles, celebrations call for mariachi music, and it's possible to drive away from Mariachi Plaza in Boyle Heights with an entire *fiesta* in your car. Mariachi music originated in Mexico. Traditional bands contain eight or more musicians, who play lively, brassy songs. For decades, mariachi musicians have gathered at the corner of First and Boyle, waiting for jobs. Dressed in tight black suits adorned with shiny silver buttons, and carrying guitars, accordions, trumpets, and big bass guitars, they're ready to go when drivers pull up to hire them for weddings, birthday parties, or *quinceañeras*, special parties for girls turning fifteen.

In the 1920s, Boyle Heights served as the center of the Jewish community. But since the 1940s, the East L.A. neighborhood has been home to a primarily Mexican-American population. Colorful murals highlight the area's mariachi traditions. The governor of Jalisco, Mexico, donated the stone *kiosko* in the plaza in 1998, honoring the links between the two countries.

Mariachi Plaza erupts in joyful celebration every November in honor of Saint Cecilia, the patron saint of music, who is especially beloved by the mariachis. People enjoy the boisterous bands and spirited dancing that goes on all day in this musical oasis in the midst of the jangling city.

High on a hill overlooking Los Angeles, the Getty Center—a college-sized campus dedicated to studying, conserving, and sharing the world's great art—attracts more than a million visitors each year to stroll through its gardens, galleries, and plazas. In its libraries, offices, and labs, scholars pore over old manuscripts, and conservation scientists develop ways to conserve art and historic sites.

The Getty Center is named for the oil tycoon J. Paul Getty, who began collecting art in 1931. By the time he died in 1976, he had built a museum in Malibu and filled it with an impressive collection of Greek, Roman, and Etruscan antiquities and French decorative arts. In his will, he left almost his entire fortune to the museum, leading to the creation of the Getty Center, which

opened in 1997, after nearly two decades of planning and construction.

At the Getty Center, a tram takes visitors far above the freeway to a plaza surrounded by buildings made of heavy stone blocks, called travertine, that are imported from Italy. Formed between eight thousand and eighty thousand years ago, the travertine contains delicate fossils of feathers, fish, leaves, and shells.

Among the Getty Center's greatest treasures is the view from the top of the hill. The city shimmers below—and on a clear day you can see snowcapped mountains, the glistening Pacific Ocean, and Catalina Island in the distance.

Shoppers fill their baskets from pyramids of sunny oranges and giant grapefruits at Farmers Market, a fantastic wonderland of little stands selling fresh produce, souvenirs, and various delicacies, located in the Fairfax district. The aromas of freshly baked pies, roasting nuts, and steaming pots of gumbo mingle—and so do tourists and locals alike.

People have loved to gather amid such abundance since the 1930s, when local farmers first trucked their fruits and vegetables to sell at bargain prices in an open field at Third and Fairfax. The idea quickly caught on, and the trucks gave way to permanent wooden stalls, shops, and cafés. At the same time, Jews from the Boyle Heights area in East Los Angeles migrated to the neighborhood, bringing with them the kosher bakeries, delicatessens, and butcher shops that soon lined Fairfax Avenue north of Farmers Market. Over the years, the Eastern European tradition has been enriched by immigrants from the Middle East, Russia, and Ethiopia. On Friday afternoons, when shoppers crowd Fairfax to buy groceries for Sabbath dinner, you can hear a host of languages. And every day, Farmers Market shoppers can now hop a trolley and ride it to a modern shopping center next door.

With the setting sun reflected on its shiny steel surfaces, the Walt Disney Concert Hall looks like a glowing spaceship that landed on Bunker Hill. Designed by architect Frank Gehry and opened in 2003, the concert hall welcomes people who come to hear music, see performances in the Roy and Edna Disney/CalArts Theater (REDCAT), or take the stairs from the sidewalk to stroll in the rooftop garden, which is actually a tiny state park.

At the beginning of the twentieth century, wealthy people built grand mansions atop Bunker Hill, but by 1920, those Angelenos had moved farther west to new, more fashionable neighborhoods, and the Victorian-style mansions on Bunker Hill were divided up into apartments and

rooming houses for poorer people hoping for better times and places ahead.

In the 1960s, the city government decided to remake Bunker Hill. It tore down the once-grand homes, sheared off the top of the steep hill, and erected a forest of glass-and-granite towers on the newly flat streets.

Now evenings on Bunker Hill are alive with art, music and theater, as dressed-up audiences hurry to the Music Center, the Disney Concert Hall, the Colburn School, and the Museum of Contemporary Art.

Far above the Pacific Ocean, the sound of friendship rings out four times a year from a windy bluff in San Pedro, a fishing and shipping community twenty miles south of downtown Los Angeles. When the seventeen-ton Korean Bell of Friendship tolls on New Year's Eve, the Fourth of July, Korean Independence Day (August 15), and Constitution Week in September, neighbors feel the rumble long after they hear the bell's low, booming tones.

The Republic of Korea gave this ornate bell and pavilion to Los Angeles in 1976 to celebrate the United States bicentennial and to honor the ties between the two countries. Los Angeles is the center of the largest Korean community outside Korea, numbering nearly a million people.

The bell, which resembles an ancient bronze bell in South Korea, commands a vast view of the Pacific all the way to Catalina Island. Twenty-seven miles across the ocean, wild boar, goats, and bison roam the grassy hills of Catalina, a wilderness preserve and vacation retreat.

Los Angeles annexed San Pedro in 1906 to gain access to its harbor. Because it was so far away, Los Angeles also added a ribbon of land known as the "Shoestring Strip" to link downtown L.A. to its new port. Today the San Pedro harbor ranks as the busiest on the West Coast.

Called the shortest railway in the world, Angels Flight first climbed the steep slope of downtown's Bunker Hill, traveling 350 feet in a little less than a minute. The two angled orange cars with black trim perform a graceful ballet during their short run, gliding over the tracks as one car goes up and the other comes down. A retired Civil War engineer, Colonel J.W. Eddy, opened this tiny railway at the dawn of the twentieth century to link the grand homes atop Bunker Hill with the shops and banks below. Residents rode up the hill for a penny instead of huffing and puffing up the steep stairs lining the street.

In the 1960s, Angels Flight was dismantled and went into storage. Unlike so many other aspects of the city, however, it returned in 1996 to ferry people up the hill from Grand Central Market to the office buildings and plazas above. Angels Flight was added to the National Register of Historic Places on October 13, 2000. After a tragic accident the next year, the railroad was shut down again, but like that famous little engine that could, it will eventually safely climb the hill again. Like a brightly colored time machine, the little railway connects Los Angeles with its past.

Peacocks roam the manicured lawns of Mission San Fernando, while water splashes in a flower-shaped fountain. Once a busy ranch and workshop that produced food, wine, blankets, and leather hides for its inhabitants and the brand-new *pueblo* of Los Angeles, now the church and restored adobe *convento* offer a look into mission life.

Mission San Fernando Rey de España was founded in 1797, the seventeenth in a chain of twenty-one missions established by Spanish friars along the coast of California in an effort to convert Native Americans to Catholicism. The priests brought the Indians from their villages to be catechized and baptized and work in the missions' fields and shops. The missions flourished, but

at a high cost. Wrenched from their culture and vulnerable to diseases from the Spaniards, the Native Americans died in large numbers during the more than seventy years of mission rule.

Earthquakes have badly damaged the mission four times since it was built in 1806. The *convento*, with its four-foot-thick walls and twenty-one arches, has survived, but the church had to be rebuilt entirely in 1974 after a large quake devastated the San Fernando Valley neighborhood. Nevertheless, it still contains furnishings from the original mission. Babies are baptized within the church's cool darkness, and modern brides and grooms exchange their vows there, just as they have for centuries.

Pasadena

Every New Year's Day, the Tournament of Roses Parade takes over the streets of Pasadena, a city that is Los Angeles' eastern neighbor. Pasadena's settlers first staged the parade in 1890 to celebrate the year-round sunshine and pleasant weather—and to gloat about it in letters and photographs to folks back home in the Midwest. The balmy weather made Pasadena a resort for rich Midwesterners, who built homes on "Millionaires' Row" along Orange Grove Avenue. Today hundreds of millions of people gather around their TVs to watch the parade of floral floats and marching bands and the Rose Bowl football game that follows. For many of them, the parade is their most enduring image of sunny Southern California.

Pasadena grew quickly after the region's first freeway opened on New Year's Eve in 1939, linking the city to downtown Los Angeles ten miles away. It became a center of scientific research, thanks to the Jet Propulsion Laboratory (JPL) and the California Institute of Technology (Caltech). At Caltech in the 1930s, seismologist Charles F. Richter developed a way to measure earthquakes, known as the Richter scale. The scientists at the world-renowned university still soothe the jittery nerves of Angelenos after every large earthquake with information about how big the shaker was, where it was centered, and along which fault it occurred.

The juicy aroma of barbecue and the playful music of steel drums pour into the streets of Leimert Park Village, a neighborhood of small businesses that has emerged as a center of African American arts and culture. Leimert Park's cafés, galleries, theaters, and nightclubs feature the work of African American artists. Several times a year, the streets and triangular village fill with artists and performers celebrating their heritage.

The curving streets were laid out in the 1920s as part of a model community designed by Olmsted and Olmsted, one of the nation's most influential architectural firms. Spanish-style homes nestled in parklike settings, and pedestrian walkways created shortcuts through the blocks.

Like many housing tracts that sprouted all over Los Angeles in the 1920s, Leimert Park was built with rules that prevented people of color from owning homes. But in the 1940s, as many African Americans came to L.A. to work in wartime industries, the restrictions began to fall. The community spread west from its traditional base along Central Avenue south of downtown. Today, a sprawling African American community finds its heart and history at Leimert Park Village.

"THE BRUIN"
Presented to The Campus
By
THE UCLA Alumni Association

There's no place book lovers would rather be each April than the Festival of Books at UCLA, where they can celebrate the joys of books and reading. They may even get a chance to talk with their favorite authors—or hug a beloved costumed character in the special children's book area. Originated by the *Los Angeles Times* in conjunction with UCLA, the Festival of Books features booths jammed full of booksellers' and publishers' latest offerings. On various stages throughout the UCLA campus, authors read from their works and discuss them.

Stately UCLA forms a majestic background for the festivities. The regal red-brick buildings rose in the late 1920s as the centerpiece of a master plan that included homes and businesses in nearby Westwood. Although one hundred years younger than most great universities, UCLA consistently ranks among the nation's top schools, and its research libraries are among the largest in the country.

Simon Wiesenthal Center

Museum of Tolerance

Dedicated to the memory of Holocaust victims, the Simon Wiesenthal Center Museum of Tolerance challenges visitors with high-tech exhibits and hands-on activities about prejudice, and videos and artifacts of injustices past and present, including the Holocaust. During the museum's construction, the city erupted in racial violence. By the time the museum opened in 1993, it included an interactive survey allowing viewers to express their opinions on racial attitudes in L.A. Today schoolchildren, police officers, teachers, and other groups tour the museum, learning valuable lessons in getting along with others in a region where more than two hundred languages are spoken and half the residents come from other countries.

1542 Explorer Juan Cabrillo sails into San Pedro Bay and notices a layer of smoke from Native American campfires hanging over the land. He names the area "Bay of Smokes." His is the first account of the effects of the "inversion layer," warm air that sits like a lid on top of the Los Angeles basin, preventing pollution from blowing away.

1769 Father Juan Crespi, on the initial Spanish expedition to what will become Los Angeles, writes the first account of an L.A. earthquake, which knocked a soldier off his horse and "lasted as long as half an 'Ave Maria.' "

1851 A young African American slave named Biddy Mason is brought by her owners to Los Angeles, where slavery is illegal. She wins freedom for her family in court and, using her wages as a nurse and midwife to acquire property, goes on to become a major downtown landowner. In 1872, she helps organize the First African Methodist Episcopal Church, the oldest African American church in the city.

1884 Writer Charles Lummis walks all the way from Cincinnati, Ohio, to Los Angeles, where he becomes city editor of the *Los Angeles Times* and later the city librarian. His enthusiastic writings lure other artists and writers to Los Angeles. He establishes the California Landmarks Club to preserve L.A.'s historic buildings and builds a stone house with his own hands, which now serves as headquarters for the Historical Society of Southern California.

1887 Los Angeles finds itself in the midst of a boom. Railroads lower fares to a dollar for a transcontinental trip to L.A. Real-estate developers tout the healthful advantages of Los Angeles' climate.

1892 Edward Doheny strikes oil. Drilling rigs sprout up throughout the region, with some areas of the city becoming virtual boomtowns. The substance that trapped Ice Age mammals forty thousand years ago creates fortunes for tycoons and for average people who were lucky enough to live in the middle of an oil field.

1904 Abbot Kinney creates Venice of America. He hopes to make it a center of fine art and music, like Venice, Italy, but finds to his dismay that his customers prefer a carnival with rides and games. Disappointed, he gives them what they want.

1909 L.A.'s first movie studios are built in the Echo Park neighborhood. Soon the Keystone Kops, the Bathing Beauties, and Laurel & Hardy film their antics outside, transforming the community of Echo Park into a huge movie set.

1913 Engineer William Mulholland opens the Los Angeles Aqueduct, bringing water from the Owens Valley to Los Angeles. As thousands of people watch, many holding tin cups to grab a taste, Mulholland opens the floodgates, gestures to the roaring water, and says, "There it is. Take it." The new water source allows developers to build housing tracts all across L.A.

1924 A film crew brings fourteen buffalo to Catalina Island to recreate the American plains for a Western movie. The crew leaves the buffalo behind. Today hundreds of their descendants roam the island's protected wilderness.

1928 Los Angeles City Hall opens. The tallest building in downtown, its unprecedented twenty-eight stories dwarf everything around it. At the top, a revolving light called the Charles Lindbergh Beacon warns low-flying planes.

1932 Los Angeles hosts the Summer Olympics in the Los Angeles Memorial Coliseum, enlarged for the occasion to seat 105,000 people. Country Club Drive becomes Olympic Boulevard in time for the event, which brings 400,000 visitors and fifty million dollars to the city.

1939 Nathanael West's *The Day of the Locust* and Raymond Chandler's *The Big Sleep* are published. Depicting a grim, desperate underside to L.A.'s sunny surface, the novels are considered definitive descriptions of L.A., continuing to influence perceptions to this day.

1942 After Japan bombs Pearl Harbor at the start of World War II, Japanese American residents of Little Tokyo are rounded up and transported to detention camps hundreds of miles away. African Americans, coming to Los Angeles, looking for wartime jobs, move into the abandoned community, one of the few places they can find housing. Little Tokyo fosters a lively nightlife, featuring Big Band music.

1951 "This is the city," intones Jack Webb at the beginning of every episode of *Dragnet*, a popular TV show based on actual cases from the Los Angeles Police Department. Airing until 1959, *Dragnet* returns eight years later for a three-year run in color.

1958 The Brooklyn Dodgers relocate to Los Angeles, bringing with them announcer Vin Scully, whose voice becomes the soundtrack to summer afternoons for generations of Angelenos. He begins every day game with "A very pleasant good afternoon to you, wherever you may be ..."

1961 The last Red Car stops running, ending an era. The Red Car trolleys had traveled on tracks throughout the L.A. area since the turn of the century, at a cost of about a penny a mile. Increasing traffic and the efforts of auto, tire, and petroleum companies usher in the age of the freeway.

1962 Dodger Stadium opens in Chavez Ravine, on April 10, with a team that includes future baseball legends Sandy Koufax, Don Drysdale, and Maury Wills. In 1963, they win the World Series.

1965 The South Los Angeles community of Watts erupts in violence and looting after police officers try to arrest a young African American motorist for drunk driving. The violence calls attention to the poverty in South Los Angeles.

1973 Tom Bradley becomes L.A.'s first African American mayor. He will lead the city for the next twenty years. During his five terms in office, the city will develop a major skyline and emerge as the leading trading partner with the Pacific Rim.

1983 "I Love L.A." by award-winning singer-songwriter Randy Newman becomes a hit heard around the world.

1984 Los Angeles becomes the first American city to host two Olympics. Although everyone fears huge traffic jams, because of efforts to organize carpools and flexible work hours, traffic flows better during the Olympics than ever before—or since.

1992 Violence, looting, and arson erupt in Los Angeles when four police officers are found not guilty of beating Rodney King, an African American man stopped for speeding. After days of unrest, King appears on television to tearfully ask, "Can we all get along?" The nearly weeklong civil strife leaves burned-out buildings throughout the city and creates a massive effort to bring economic development to the inner city.

1994 On January 17 at 4:31 A.M., the Northridge earthquake strikes with a magnitude of 6.8, killing more than sixty people, injuring more than six thousand others, and destroying or seriously damaging more than a thousand buildings. Freeway overpasses collapse and more than twenty thousand people lose their homes in one of the costliest disasters in American history.

2002 WNBA center Lisa Leslie executes the first slam dunk by a woman in a professional basketball game. Leslie, who grew up in Compton and Inglewood and graduated from USC, performed her feat for the Los Angeles Sparks at the Staples Center in downtown L.A.

2005 Antonio Villaraigosa is elected mayor of Los Angeles, becoming the city's first Latino mayor since Cristobal Aguilar in 1872.

2007 A fire breaks out in Griffith Park, burning eight hundred acres of the rugged hillside before firefighters bring it under control. Miraculously, no landmark structures are harmed, but hiking destinations Dante's View and Captain's Roost are burned. Volunteers and city officials vow to restore them.

City of Angels
In and Around Los Angeles

Text copyright © 1999, 2008 by Julie Jaskol and Brian Lewis / Illustrations copyright © 1999, 2008 by Elisa Kleven

Designed by Amy Inouye, www.futurestudio.com

10 9 8 7 6 5 4 3 2 1

ISBN-13 978-1-883318-85-7 / ISBN-10 1-883318-85-8

LIBRARY OF CONGRESS CATALOGING-IN-PUBLICATION DATA

Jaskol, Julie.
  City of angels : in and around Los Angeles / by Julie Jaskol & Brian Lewis; illustrated by Elisa Kleven.
  p. cm.
  ISBN 9781883318857 (hardcover : alk. paper)
1. Historic sites—California—Los Angeles Region—Juvenile literature. 2. Historic buildings—California—Los Angeles Region—Juvenile literature. 3. Ethnic neighborhoods—California—Los Angeles Region—Juvenile literature. 4. Los Angeles Region (Calif.)—History, Local—Juvenile literature. 5. Los Angeles Region (Calif.)—Description and travel—Juvenile literature. 6. Los Angeles (Calif.)—Description and travel—Juvenile literature.
I. Title.

F869.L86 A2 +
979.4'94-dc21

2008030301

Printed in China

ANGEL CITY PRESS
2118 Wilshire Blvd. #880
Santa Monica, California 90403
310.395.9982
www.angelcitypress.com

On the front cover: When the Los Angeles Central Library opened in 1927, its architect boasted that the building could withstand both earthquakes and fires. Unfortunately, the books couldn't. In 1986 two fires destroyed 800,000 books and damaged 800,000 others. A massive volunteer effort saved nearly all the damaged books by painstakingly freezing them and then treating each volume rescued from the blaze. The building, which was virtually undamaged, reopened in 1993 with a new wing. With two and a half million books, recordings, and other materials, the L.A. Central Library is the largest research library west of the Mississippi. A welcoming inscription over the entrance proclaims, "Books invite all, they constrain none."